SneakerBlossom

Study Guide

for

Black Ships Before Troy

by Rosemary Sutcliff

also published as *The Iliad* by Rosemary Sutcliff

Complete Edition

by Lisa Pelissier

www.sneakerblossom.com

Scripture quotations taken from the (NASB®) New American Standard Bible®,
Copyright © 1960, 1971, 1977, 1995 by The Lockman Foundation.
Used by permission. All rights reserved. www.lockman.org

Table of Contents

About 5

Introduction.. 9

Student Chapter 1: The Golden Apple 13

Student Chapter 2: Ship Gathering 15

Student Chapter 3: Quarrel with the High King 17

Student Chapter 4: Single Combat 19

Student Chapter 5: The Women of Troy 20

Student Chapter 6: The High King's Embassy 22

Student Chapter 7: The Horses of King Rhesus 24

Student Chapter 8: Red Rain 26

Student Chapter 9: Battle for the Ships.................................... 27

Student Chapter 10: The Armor of Achilles 29

Student Chapter 11: Vengeance for Patroclus 31

Student Chapter 12: Funeral Games 33

Student Chapter 13: Ransom for Hector 35

Student Chapter 14: The Luck of Troy 37

Student Chapter 15 Warrior Women 39

Student Chapter 16: The Death of Achilles 40

Student Chapter 17: Poisoned Arrow 42

Student Chapter 18: The Wooden Horse 44

Student Chapter 19: The Fall of Troy 46

Student Index of Characters.. 49

Student Map Work.. 56

Teacher Chapter 1: The Golden Apple 63

Teacher Chapter 2: Ship Gathering 67

Teacher Chapter 3: Quarrel with the High King 70

Teacher Chapter 4: Single Combat 75

Teacher Chapter 5: The Women of Troy 78

Teacher Chapter 6: The High King's Embassy 81

Teacher Chapter 7: The Horses of King Rhesus 84

Teacher Chapter 8: Red Rain 87

Teacher Chapter 9: Battle for the Ships.................... 89

Teacher Chapter 10: The Armor of Achilles 92

Teacher Chapter 11: Vengeance for Patroclus 95

Teacher Chapter 12: Funeral Games 99

Teacher Chapter 13: Ransom for Hector 102

Teacher Chapter 14: The Luck of Troy 104

Teacher Chapter 15 Warrior Women 107

Teacher Chapter 16: The Death of Achilles 109

Teacher Chapter 17: Poisoned Arrow 112

Teacher Chapter 18: The Wooden Horse 115

Teacher Chapter 19: The Fall of Troy 118

Teacher Index of Characters...................................... 123

Teacher Map Work.. 130

Relaxed Workbook Answer Key.................................. 134

SneakerBlossom Study Guides are four things:
Christian, Classical, Versatile, Affordable*

Christian: Every SneakerBlossom Study Guide functions not only as a guide to comprehension of the work being studied, but as a course in the Christian worldview.

Classical: SneakerBlossom Study Guides encourage students to study the great books of history in a manner appropriate to the student's capacity. Great emphasis is placed on contemplating virtue, truth, and beauty.

Versatile: SneakerBlossom Study Guides are available in many different formats that can be used from younger children through high school. They can be used in a homeschool setting or in a classroom setting.

Affordable: SneakerBlossom Study Guides can be used by the whole family. Purchase just the answer key and do the work aloud and you need only buy one book. Purchase a complete edition and use your own paper. Again, with only one book you have a study for the whole family.

SneakerBlossom Study Guides are available in several formats

Complete: Comprehension and discussion/essay questions at the front for the student, and comprehension and discussion questions and answers at the back for parents and teachers. Includes complete lists of Level A, Level B, and Level C character indexing and map work. If you can only buy one study guide, this is the one you want. This is the "use your own paper" or "do it out loud" version. Available in print version only.

Answer Key: Includes all comprehension and discussion/essay questions and answers. Also includes complete lists of Level A, Level B, and Level C character indexing and map work. This is the version to buy in order to grade the workbooks. You can also use the answer key if you are doing everything orally. Available in print and digital versions.

Relaxed Student Workbook: All comprehension questions are asked in a simple format, such as fill-in-the-blank or multiple choice. Character index is limited to main characters and well-known historical figures. Includes basic map work. Discussion/essay questions are not included. Available in print version only.

Studious Student Workbook: All comprehension questions have lines for students to write answers. Character index lists main characters and minor characters. Includes map work. Discussion/essay questions are not included. Available in print version only.

Scholarly Student Workbook: All comprehension questions have lines for students to write answers. Discussion/essay questions are included so that students can contemplate answers and write essays if desired. Character index includes every character mentioned in the text. Includes map work. Available in print version only.

Comfortable Student Workbook: Dyslexia-friendly font. All comprehension questions have multiple-choice answers. Discussion/essay questions are included. Indexing is cut-and-paste.

Questions Only: Includes all comprehension and discussion/essay questions as well as a list of characters and locations. Available in digital version only.

SneakerBlossom Study Guides are easy to use.

1) Read the Book: Have the students read a chapter of the book, or read it to them.

2) Comprehension Questions: Answer the comprehension questions for each chapter. You can do this aloud with your students. You can purchase student workbooks and have your students do the work on their own. You can purchase the complete guide and have the students do the work on their own using a separate sheet of paper.

3) Discussion Questions: After comprehension questions are done, discuss one or more of the given topics with the students. Let the discussion be spontaneous and serendipitous. Don't feel that you need to address every discussion question given. If you have a good discussion then you've succeeded.

4) Character Index: A character index is given at the back of each student study guide as well as in the complete guide and the answer key. For each chapter read, students can fill out information in the index about the newly introduced characters in that chapter. They can use the index for reference as they read the book. The Character Index is leveled. **Never force anyone to do a Level C index.** Some students will take great joy in recording information about every single character. For other students this will be torture. There is no reason to torture them. It's there for the kids who find it a joyful exercise.

5) Map Work: Map work is included at the back of each study guide. Maps in PDF format can be obtained by emailing **sneakerblossom@yahoo.com**

Additional Thoughts

Comprehension Questions

In my opinion, comprehension questions exist to help the child remember what they read, and also to help the teacher verify that the child has read the material. It is up to you whether or not you require the answers in complete sentences. If you have a child that always remembers everything they read, just read and discuss: don't bother with comprehension questions at all. It's up to you. Your goal is not the make your child memorize the contents of the text. Your goal is to make your child love learning. A child who loves learning becomes an adult who continues learning over the course of his or her life. Your goal should be to help your child love God and to live a life full of virtue, truth, and beauty. Use the book and the SneakerBlossom Study Guides in your efforts toward that end.

Discussion Questions

Please note that my answers to discussion questions are only a starting place. They are not "the right answer". Your discussions may take an entirely different path.

Introduction: What is the *Iliad?*

Black Ships Before Troy by Rosemary Sutcliff is a retelling of the classic tale, the *Iliad*. The *Iliad* was written by Homer, an ancient Greek poet. It is generally considered to be the first work of Western literature, written in the 8th century BC. The *Iliad* tells the story of Achilles during the Trojan War. It begins with the disagreement between Agamemnon and Achilles and ends with the restoration of the body of Hector to his father, Priam. *Black Ships Before Troy* tells the full story of the Trojan War, using other sources from ancient literature to fill in the events before and after the events described in Homer's *Iliad*.

Homer also wrote the *Odyssey*, which tells the story of Odysseus' journey back to Ithaca after the Trojan War. Virgil wrote the *Aeneid*, which tells the story of the Trojan Aeneas' journey as he left a fallen Troy and sought to establish a new city, which became Rome. The story of the Trojan horse is part of the *Aeneid*.

The *Iliad*, the *Odyssey*, and the *Aeneid* are foundational works to ancient Greek and Roman culture and to all of Western civilization.

The Trojan War – Taking Sides

The war started with an apple labeled "To the Fairest". Paris, a Trojan, chose Aphrodite. In so doing, he rejected Hera and Athene, setting the stage not only for the battle between Greece and Troy, but a war that became a man-sized chess game amongst the gods.

Gods for Greece:

Athene, Hephaestus, Hera, Hermes, Poseidon, Thetis

Prominent Greek Warriors:

Achilles, Agamemnon, Diomedes, Menelaus, Odysseus

Gods for Troy:

Aphrodite, Apollo, Ares, Zeus

Prominent Trojan Warriors:

Hector, Paris

NOTE: Other characters have additional impact in the Iliad *that are not listed here. The characters listed above are the characters that are featured as main characters in* Black Ships Before Troy.

Student Question Section

Chapter 1: The Golden Apple

Characters Introduced in this Chapter

> Level A: Aphrodite, Athene, Helen, Hera, Menelaus,
>
> Odysseus, Paris, Priam, Zeus,
>
> Level B: Eris, Oenone, Penelope, Thetis
>
> Level C: Hecuba, Peleus, Helen's baby daughter

Map Work:

> Level A: Aegean Sea, Black Sea, Greece, Sparta, Troy
>
> Level B: Ithaca, Olympus
>
> Level C: Ida

Comprehension Questions

Q1: Where did the golden apple come from?

Q2: Who wanted the apple?

Q3: What happened to Paris when he was a baby? Why?

Q4: What kind of a person is Paris?

Q5: What did the goddesses ask Paris to do?

Q6: What made Paris choose Aphrodite?

Q7: Who was the most beautiful woman in the world? Who was
her husband?

Q8: What did Paris and Helen do?

<u>Suggested Lines of Discussion to Pursue</u>

DQ1: How do the gods interact with mankind in this chapter?

DQ2: What do the Greeks believe about their gods?

DQ3: How are the Greek gods different from the God of the Bible?

DQ4: The story says Oenone is a "wood nymph". What is a nymph
in Greek mythology?

Chapter 2: Ship Gathering

Characters Introduced in this Chapter

      Level A: Achilles, Agamemnon

      Level B: Ajax, Calchas, Chiron, Diomedes, Hephaestus,

          Patroclus

      Level C: Idomeneus, Lycomedes, Nestor

Map Work

      Level A: Crete

      Level B: Mycenae

      Level C: Argos, Aulis Harbor, Pylos, Pytho, Salamis,

          Scyros, Thessaly, Thisbe, River Styx (not on map)

Comprehension Questions and Answers

Q1: Why is the league of Greeks setting out to attack Troy?

Q2: Who are Achilles' parents? What is unusual about his mother?

Q3: Why is Thetis afraid for Achilles?

Q4: How did Thetis try to keep Achilles out of the war?

Q5: What trick did Odysseus play? Why?

Suggested Lines of Discussion to Pursue

DQ1: Achilles' mother dipped him into the river Styx in order to grant him immortality. Do you think this was a moral act (a right thing to do)? Would you pursue immortality in this way if it were an option?

DQ2: The Greek kings went to fight with Menelaus because they had alliances with him. Is it always right to fight on behalf of a friend, just because you are friends?

Chapter 3: Quarrel with the High King

Characters Introduced in this Chapter

Level A: Apollo, Chryseis, Hector

Level B: Briseis

Level C: Chryseis' father, Protesilaus

Comprehension Questions

Q1: How long did the Greeks camp outside Troy?

Q2: What were they doing during all that time?

Q3: Why did the Greeks believe that sickness came upon them?

Q4: Whose side was Athene on? Aphrodite?

Q5: Why were Achilles and Agamemnon fighting?

Q6: What did Achilles pray for?

Suggested Lines of Discussion to Pursue

Discussion Note: Homer's *Iliad* begins with this part of the story.
The parts of *Black Ships Before Troy* that come before this
were written in other ancient Greek texts.

DQ1: What do we learn about the Greeks' beliefs about their gods
in this chapter? How do these things compare to the
Christian's beliefs about God?

DQ2: Agamemnon sends cattle for a sacrifice to appease Apollo. How is this like Bible sacrifices? How is it different?

DQ3: Achilles prays for his own people to lose the war, in order to assuage his drive for vengeance against Agamemnon. Was this the right thing to do? Is there ever a circumstance where turning against your own people would be the right thing to do?

DQ4: The Greeks, including Agamemnon, are fighting because Paris stole Menelaus' wife. Do you find it hypocritical that Agamemnon then steals Briseis from Achilles? Does it make a difference that she isn't his wife, but only his servant girl whom he loves?

Chapter 4: Single Combat

Characters Introduced in this Chapter

Level B: Thersites

Comprehension Questions

Q1: What did Zeus give Agamemnon?

Q2: How were they going to end the conflict?

Q3: What does Aphrodite do in the duel?

Q4: Who won the duel? Why?

Q5: What is Helen's response when Paris shows up after the duel?

Q6: What did Aphrodite do to Helen?

Q7: Why did Aphrodite want Helen to stay with Paris?

Suggested Lines of Discussion to Pursue

DQ1: Was Odysseus right to tell the army that it was shameful to leave after such a long siege? Or were the men right to want to go home?

DQ2: In the beginning of the chapter, Zeus gave Agamemnon a false dream. In the Bible, does God ever give people dreams? Are they ever false dreams?

Chapter 5: The Women of Troy

Characters Introduced in this Chapter

Level A: Hades

Level B: Aeneas, Andromache, Machaon

Level C: Astyanax, Pandarus, Sarpedon

Comprehension Questions

Q1: Why did the war keep going after the duel was over?

Q2: Who was winning the battle before the Trojan soothsayer came to Hector?

Q3: Why doesn't Hector want to make a sacrifice to the gods?

Q4: What is Paris doing during the battle? What is his excuse?

Q5: What is Helen's response to Paris' delay?

Q6: Why did Hector go to find his wife before returning to the battle?

Q7: What does Hector believe will happen to Troy? To Andromache?

Suggested Lines of Discussion to Pursue

DQ1: Hector does not want to make a sacrifice to the gods while he is still dirty from battle. What does this tell us about the Greek attitude toward their gods? Should Christians also have this attitude?

DQ2: Is Helen right to disrespect Paris as cowardly for not wanting to go into battle? Is it always cowardly to avoid war?

Chapter 6: The High King's Embassy

Characters Introduced in this Chapter

    Level C: Phoenix

Comprehension Questions

Q1: Why did Athene decide to stop the fighting?

Q2: Who is the "High King"?

Q3: Which two men were selected for single combat?

Q4: Who won the duel?

Q5: Why were the Greeks unable to conquer the Trojans when the fighting began again?

Q6: What did Agamemnon want to do? Why?

Q7: What alternate plan was suggested by Nestor?

Q8: What was Achilles' reply to the request that the others make of him?

Suggested Lines of Discussion to Pursue

DQ1: After the duel, Hector and Ajax exchanged gifts, and it seems
that both esteemed each other greatly. What does this tell
us about the values that the ancient Greeks and Trojans
held?   Do you think this is a good way to think about the
opposing side in a war?

DQ2: Phoenix urges Achilles to be a great enough man to let go of
his anger when forgiveness has been asked and restitution
paid. He says the anger was only appropriate while the
injury remained. What does this tell us about how the
Greeks viewed revenge?

Chapter 7: The Horses of King Rhesus

Characters Introduced in this Chapter

> Level C: Dolon, Rhesus

Map Work

> Level C: Thrace

Comprehension Questions

Q1: What plan did Menelaus and the council instigate, in order to learn what the next day would hold?

Q2: Who will carry out Menelaus' plan?

Q3: What plan did Hector begin at the same time? Who answered his request?

Q4: What animal are Diomedes and Odysseus compared to? What about Dolon?

Q5: What happens to Dolon?

Q6: What did Odysseus and Diomedes do with the information they learned from Dolon?

Suggested Lines of Discussion to Pursue

DQ1: Was it fair for Diomedes to kill Dolon after Dolon had told him
everything he wanted to know?

DQ2: Diomedes and Odysseus kill King Rhesus and his twelve
companions while they are sleeping soundly. Did this
bother you? Is there a moral difference between killing
during a battle and killing sleeping men during a raid on the
enemy camp?

Chapter 8: Red Rain

<u>Characters Introduced in this Chapter</u>

Level B: Pan

Level C: Eurypolus, Hecamede

<u>Comprehension Questions</u>

Q1: What strange phenomenon happens? Who does it happen to?
Why?

Q2: Why are shepherds quiet at noon?

Q3: What happened to Agamemnon in the battle?

Q4: What happened to Diomedes in the battle? Odysseus?

Q5: Why are the Greeks particularly worried when Machaon is
wounded?

Q6: Why did Achilles send Patroclus to Nestor?

Q7: What idea does Nestor give Patroclus?

<u>Suggested Lines of Discussion to Pursue</u>

DQ1: Who is Pan and why would the shepherds fear rousing him?

DQ2: Should Achilles have joined the Greeks in fighting, despite his
grudge against Agamemnon?

Chapter 9: Battle for the Ships

Characters Introduced in this Chapter

> Level A: Poseidon
>
> Level C: Asios, Glaucus, Helenus

Map Work

> Level C: Xanthus River

Comprehension Questions

Q1: In the opening scene of this chapter, what are the Trojans trying to do?

Q2: Why do the Trojans think that Zeus is against them? How does Hector refute this?

Q3: What assistance does Zeus give the Trojans?

Q4: What does Zeus do after he helps the Trojans?

Q5: What god intervenes next? Over what natural things does he rule? What does he do?

Q6: Who is injured in the Greek charge?

Q7: What does Zeus do when he sees the injured man?

Q8: What does the revived Hector do?

<u>Suggested Lines of Discussion to Pursue</u>

DQ1: Do the Trojans heed the evil omen of the red snake and stop fighting? Why? What does this tell you about what they think about their gods?

DQ2: What do we learn about the Greek gods in this chapter? Contrast these things with the characteristics of the God of the Bible.

Chapter 10: The Armor of Achilles

Characters Introduced in this Chapter

> Level B: Automedon, the West Wind
>
> Level C: Balius, Death, Pedasus, Sleep, Xanthus

Comprehension Questions

Q1: Why does Achilles taunt Patroclus?

Q2: Why is Achilles grieved?

Q3: What is unusual about the two horses, Xanthus and Balius?

Q4: What does Patroclus do?

Q5: Who does Achilles pray to? What is his prayer?

Q6: What happens to Sarpedon?

Q7: Why didn't Patroclus return to Achilles right away as he promised?

Q8: What happens to Patroclus? What does he prophesy?

Q9: Who wants the body of Patroclus? Why?

Q10: Who remains unmoving beside the body of Patroclus? What happens to them?

Q11: Who is winning the battle at the end of this chapter?

Suggested Lines of Discussion to Pursue

DQ1: Achilles was grieved because his vow prevented him from fighting. What does Achilles' grief demonstrate about the values of the Greeks? Is it ever right to break a vow?

DQ2: What does the story of the death of Sarpedon tell us about the gods?

Chapter 11: Vengeance for Patroclus

Characters Introduced in this Chapter

      Level C: Antilochus

Comprehension Questions

Q1: What does Antilochus tell Achilles?

Q2: Why does Thetis tell Achilles not to go into battle yet? What is
she going to do?

Q3: Who ended up with the body of Patroclus? How did this come
about?

Q4: Describe or draw the armor Hephaestus makes for Achilles.

Q5: Why does Odysseus delay Achilles' return to battle?

Q6: Who gives Achilles a prophecy? What is that prophecy?

Q7: What is Hector's fate? What does he request?

Q8: What does Achilles do with Hector's body?

Suggested Lines of Discussion to Pursue

DQ1: Do some research to learn more about the shield of Achilles.
It is said to represent a microcosm of the Iliad itself. Online
resources are plentiful.

DQ2: What do we learn about the Greeks' values because of Odysseus' decision to have Achilles make peace with Agamemnon before returning to battle?

DQ3: The goddess Hera gives a prophecy through the horse Xanthus that Achilles' death is near. What does this tell us about the Greek gods? Does the God of the Bible share these qualities?

DQ4: Does Achilles do right by showing no mercy to Hector in the end? By refusing to assure him that he will return his body to his father as he is dying? Does he bring about his own doom by his lack of mercy? Or would Paris have killed him anyway?

DQ5: In chapter 3, we see Achilles praying for the Greeks to lose the war. Does Achilles bear some responsibility for the death of Patroclus?

Chapter 12: Funeral Games

Characters Introduced in this Chapter

Level C: Epeius, Eumelus, Euryalus, Meriones

Comprehension Questions

Q1: Why is Andromache sad?

Q2: Why does Andromache believe that Hector will not proceed to the next life in Hades?

Q3: What vision does Achilles have?

Q4: Describe the ceremonies that were given to usher Patroclus into the next world.

Q5: What does Achilles do as a result of his violent grief?

Q6: What do the gods think about this?

Suggested Lines of Discussion to Pursue

DQ1: Andromache believes that without a proper burial, the dead have to wander in the borderlands between the living and the dead. What does this tell us about the Greek beliefs about the gods and the afterlife? Compare this to the Christian beliefs about life after death.

DQ2: What does Achilles' vision of Patroclus tell us about the Greeks' beliefs?

DQ3: Apollo protects Hector's body from further harm by Achilles. What does this tell us about the Greek gods?

Chapter 13: Ransom for Hector

Characters Introduced in this Chapter

 Level A: Hermes

 Level B: Iris

 Level C: Deiphobos

Comprehension Questions

Q1: How did the gods persuade Achilles to stop abusing the body of Hector?

Q2: What message did Iris take to Priam?

Q3: What help did Hermes give to Priam?

Q4: What are some of Hector's good qualities that the mourners enumerate?

Q5: How was the funeral of Hector different from the funeral of Patroclus?

Suggested Lines of Discussion to Pursue

DQ1: Of the heroes in the book, Odysseus, Achilles, and Hector, who is your favorite? Why?

DQ2: Did Achilles change from the spoiled, immature boy into a gracious and mature man with his new willingness to return Hector's body to Priam? Or was he only trying to please his mother and the gods, whom he feared in their anger toward him?

Discussion Note: Homer's *Iliad* ends here, with the return of Hector's body and before the death of Achilles. The story of the Trojan horse is found in Virgil's *Aeneid*. The Aeneid is the story of the Trojan Aeneas and how he founded Rome.

Chapter 14: The Luck of Troy

Characters Introduced in this Chapter

>Level B: Memnon, Penthesilea

>Level C: Thrasymedes, a queen of Egypt, the king of Delos

Map Work

>Level C: Delos

Comprehension Questions

Q1: Why is the war at a standstill?

Q2: What was the Palladium?

Q3: What plan does Odysseus devise?

Q4: Why did the Greeks kick the beggar out of their camp?

Q5: How did the beggar get Helen to take care of him?

Q6: Who was the beggar?

Q7: How did Odysseus manage to steal the Palladium?

Suggested Lines of Discussion to Pursue

DQ1: Does Odysseus believe that the power of Athene rests with the Palladium? Why do you think that?

DQ2: Did you know all along that the beggar was Odysseus? What clues did you have?

DQ3: Why do you think that Odysseus chose to reveal himself to Helen, when he might has stayed disguised as a beggar?

Chapter 15: Warrior Women

Characters Introduced in this Chapter

> Level A: Ares

> Level C: Hippolyta

Map Work

> Level C: River Thermodon

Comprehension Questions

Q1: Who are the Amazons?

Q2: Why did Penthesilea decide to become a warrior?

Q3: What happened to the Amazons?

Suggested Lines of Discussion to Pursue

DQ1: Did the Greeks and the Trojans treat the women soldiers differently than they treated men soldiers?

DQ2: Is it appropriate for women to fight in wars?

DQ3: Was the Amazon River named after the Amazon women, or were the women named after the river?

Chapter 16: The Death of Achilles

Characters Introduced in this Chapter

      Level A: Dionysus

      Level C: Polydamas

Comprehension Questions

Q1: Why were the Trojans hiding out inside the walls of Troy?

Q2: What suggestion does Polydamas make?

Q3: Why does Polydamas' suggestion make Paris angry?

Q4: Who does Memnon kill first?

Q5: Who kills Memnon?

Q6: What prevented the Greeks from taking Troy that day?

Q7: What do they do with Achilles' ashes?

Q8: What becomes of Achilles' armor?

Q9: Why did the Trojan prisoners pick Odysseus?

Q10: What becomes of Ajax?

Suggested Lines of Discussion to Pursue

DQ1: What do we learn about the Greek gods from the example of
    Dionysus?

DQ2: Is it better to be dead or to be in disgrace? Why?

DQ3: Was it annoying that the title of the chapter was a spoiler,
    "The Death of Achilles"?

DQ4: Achilles dies in the midst of a great battle, but he dies from an
    arrow shot from above. Paris is not fighting in the midst of
    the warriors, but is shooting arrows from the gate-tower. Is
    this characteristic of Paris? How?

Chapter 17: Poisoned Arrow

<u>Characters Introduced in this Chapter</u>

Level A: Heracles

Level B: the Fates, Philoctetes

<u>Map Work</u>

Level C: Lemnos

<u>Comprehension Questions</u>

Q1: What does the soothsayer Calchas advise the Greeks to do?

Q2: Who is Philoctetes?

Q3: What power does Philoctetes possess that will enable him to help them?

Q4: Who does Philoctetes shoot?

Q5: Who does Paris flee to for comfort? What excuse does he give her?

Q6: How does she respond to his pleas?

<u>Suggested Lines of Discussion to Pursue</u>

DQ1: Philoctetes was abandoned by the Greeks, and then rescued because they wanted to use him. What do you think he is feeling now?

DQ2: Do the Greeks believe they are responsible for their actions when the gods have intervened? Contrast Ajax with Paris.

DQ3: Oenone first rejects Paris' pleas for help. Paris had abandoned her for another woman ten years earlier and she felt she owed him nothing. Then, after he has died, she chooses to die with him for the sake of their love. What do you think about Oenone's decisions? Was dying with Paris a beautiful expression of love or a foolish waste of a life?

Chapter 18: The Wooden Horse

Characters Introduced in this Chapter

Level A: Cassandra

Level B: Laocoön, Sinon

Level C: Palamedes, Laocoön's sons

Map Work

Level C: Tenedos

Comprehension Questions

Q1: What recommendation does Calchas give the Greeks?

Q2: Where does Odysseus get his good idea?

Q3: What story was to be told to the Trojans to explain the presence of a giant horse?

Q4: How many men could fit in the belly of the horse?

Q5: Who warns the Trojans against the horse? Why don't they heed the warning?

Q6: What did the sea serpents do? What did the Trojans infer from that?

Q7: Besides Laocoön, who warns the Trojans against the horse?

Suggested Lines of Discussion to Pursue

DQ1: Were the Trojans dumb to take the horse into the city? How did their belief in the gods affect that decision?

.

DQ2: Why didn't the Greeks return the Luck of Troy along with the gift of the horse? After all, their contention was that the horse was an offering to Athene to appease her wrath over the theft of the Luck of Troy. Wouldn't that have made Sinon's story more believable?

Chapter 19: The Fall of Troy

Comprehension Questions

Q1: What sign did the Greeks on the ships send to Sinon? What

sign did Sinon give those inside the horse?

Q2: What happened to Priam? To the queen and princesses?

Q3: What request does Odysseus make of Menelaus? Why?

Q4: What happens to Helen in the end?

Suggested Lines of Discussion to Pursue

DQ1: What does this chapter tell us about the value the Greeks

placed on keeping promises?

Extra Discussion Questions

DQ1: How is Paris' end in his beginning?

DQ2: Would the story have played out differently if Paris had chosen Athene (wisdom) or Hera (power) as the recipient of the apple?

DQ3: The gods influence the story from beginning to end. Is it fair to hold the characters responsible for their actions?

DQ4: Who was the most righteous character in this book? Why? Who was the most villainous? Why?

DQ5: Discuss the flow of Achilles' life. Was he a righteous man or an unrighteous one?

DQ6: Which side represents the "good guys" in this story? Was this a just war? How do we define a just war?

DQ7: How did anger lead the Greeks into destruction? How do we see anger in our culture now (eg: the internet!) and how is it affecting us as a people?

DQ8: How does our sin affect others? Consider Achilles in his anger refusing to fight.

DQ9: Given the choice, would you choose a short life with glory, like Achilles and Hector, or a long life with no glory, like all the Greeks who never got into an epic tale?

DQ10: Did you enjoy this book? Why or why not?

Index of characters – Level A

Write descriptions of each character as you read the book

Character	Chapter	Type
Achilles	2	demigod
Agamemnon	2	man
Aphrodite	1	goddess
Apollo	3	god
Ares	15	god
Athene	1	goddess
Cassandra	18	woman
Chryseis	3	woman
Dionysus	16	god
Hades	5	god
Hector	3	man
Helen	1	woman
Hera	1	goddess
Heracles	17	demigod
Hermes	13	god
Menelaus	1	man
Odysseus	1	man
Paris	1	man
Poseidon	9	god
Priam	1	man
Zeus	1	god

Index of characters – Level B

Write descriptions of each character as you read the book

Character	Chapter	Type
Achilles	2	demigod
Aeneas	5	man
Agamemnon	2	man
Ajax	2	man
Andromache	5	woman
Aphrodite	1	goddess
Apollo	3	god
Ares	15	god
Athene	1	goddess
Automedon	10	man
Briseis	3	woman
Calchas	2	man
Cassandra	18	woman
Chiron	2	centaur
Chryseis	3	woman
Diomedes	2	man
Dionysus	16	god
Eris	1	goddess
Fates	17	other
Hades	5	god
Hector	3	man
Helen	1	woman
Hephaestus	2	god
Hera	1	goddess
Heracles	17	demigod
Hermes	13	god
Iris	13	goddess
Laocoön	18	man

Character	Chapter	Type
Machaon	5	man
Memnon	14	man
Menelaus	1	man
Odysseus	1	man
Oenone	1	nymph
Pan	8	god
Paris	1	man
Patroclus	2	man
Penelope	1	woman
Penthesilea	14	woman
Philoctetes	17	man
Poseidon	9	god
Priam	1	man
Sinon	18	man
Thersites	4	man
Thetis	1	nymph
West Wind	10	god
Zeus	1	god

Index of characters – Level C

Write descriptions of each character as you read the book

Character	Chapter	Type
Achilles	2	demigod
Aeneas	5	man
Agamemnon	2	man
Ajax	2	man
Andromache	5	woman
Antilochus	11	man
Aphrodite	1	goddess
Apollo	3	god
Ares	15	god
Asios	9	man
Astyanax	5	man
Athene	1	goddess
Automedon	10	man
Balius	10	horse
Briseis	3	woman
Calchas	2	man
Cassandra	18	woman
Chiron	2	centaur
Chryseis	3	woman
Chryseis' Father	3	man
Death	10	god
Deiphobos	13	man
Diomedes	2	man

Character	Chapter	Type
Dionysus	16	god
Dolon	7	man
Epeius	12	man
Eris	1	goddess
Eumelus	12	man
Euryalus	12	man
Eurypolus	8	man
Fates	17	other
Glaucus	9	man
Hades	5	god
Hecamede	8	woman
Hector	3	man
Hecuba	1	woman
Helen	1	woman
Helen's baby	1	woman
Helenus	9	man
Hephaestus	2	god
Hera	1	goddess
Heracles	17	demigod
Hermes	13	god
Hippolyta	15	demigod
Idomeneus	2	man
Iris	13	goddess
King of Delos	14	man
Laocoön	18	man

Character	Chapter	Type
Laocoön's sons	18	man
Lycomedes	2	man
Machaon	5	man
Memnon	14	man
Menelaus	1	man
Meriones	12	man
Nestor	2	man
Odysseus	1	man
Oenone	1	nymph
Palamedes	18	man
Pan	8	god
Pandarus	5	man
Paris	1	man
Patroclus	2	man
Pedasus	10	horse
Peleus	1	man
Penelope	1	woman
Penthesilea	14	woman
Philoctetes	17	man
Phoenix	6	man
Polydamas	16	man
Poseidon	9	god
Priam	1	man
Protesilaus	3	man

Character	Chapter	Type
Queen of Egypt	14	woman
Rhesus	7	man
Sarpedon	5	man
Sinon	18	man
Sleep	10	god
Thersites	4	man
Thetis	1	nymph
Thrasymedes	14	man
West Wind	10	god
Xanthus	10	horse
Zeus	1	god

Level A Map Work

# on Map	Place	Chapter	Instructions
1	Aegean Sea	1	Draw blue waves on the Aegean Sea.
2	Black Sea	1	Draw black waves on the Black Sea.
3	Crete	2	Color Crete yellow.
4	Greece	1	Shade Greece orange.
5	Sparta	1	Circle Sparta in red.
6	Troy	1	Draw a horse near Troy.

Ancient Greece

Level B Map Work

# on Map	Place	Chapter	Instructions
1	Aegean Sea	1	Draw blue waves on the Aegean Sea.
2	Black Sea	1	Draw black waves on the Black Sea.
3	Crete	2	Color Crete yellow.
4	Greece	1	Shade Greece orange.
5	Ithaca	1	Color Ithaca blue.
6	Mycenae	2	Circle Mycenae in purple.
7	Olympus	1	Draw a mountain.
8	Sparta	1	Circle Sparta in red.
9	Troy	1	Draw a horse near Troy.

Ancient Greece

Level C Map Work

# on Map	Place	Chapter	Instructions
1	Aegean Sea	1	Draw blue waves on the Aegean Sea.
2	Argos	2	Circle Argos in green.
3	Aulis Harbor	2	Color the water blue.
4	Black Sea	1	Draw black waves on the Black Sea.
5	Crete	2	Color Crete yellow.
6	Delos	14	Circle Delos in brown.
7	Greece	1	Shade Greece orange.
8	Ida	1	Draw a mountain.
9	Ithaca	1	Color Ithaca blue.
10	Lemnos	17	Color Lemnos pink.
11	Mycenae	2	Circle Mycenae in purple.
12	Olympus	1	Draw a mountain.
13	Pylos	2	Circle Pylos in gray.
14	Pytho	2	Circle Pytho in light brown.
15	River Thermodon	15	Draw a blue arrow toward Pytho.
16	Salamis	2	Color Salamis magenta.
17	Scyros	2	Color Scyros lime green.
18	Sparta	1	Circle Sparta in red.
19	Tenedos	18	Color Tenedos blue.
20	Thessaly	2	Shade Thessaly light red.
21	Thisbe	2	Circle Thisbe in teal.
22	Thrace	7	Shade Thrace yellow.
23	Troy	1	Draw a horse near Troy.
24	Xanthus River	9	Trace the river in blue.

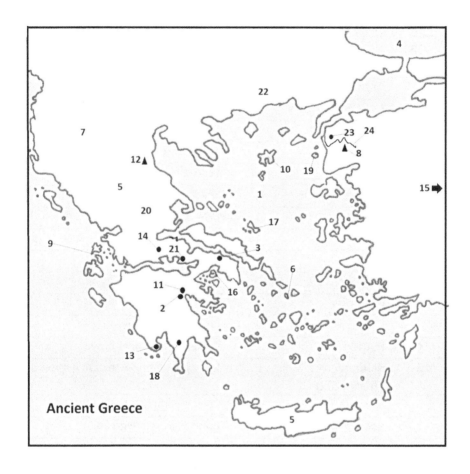

Ancient Greece

Teacher Question & Answer Section

Chapter 1: The Golden Apple

Characters Introduced in this Chapter

>Level A: Aphrodite, Athene, Helen, Hera, Menelaus,
>
>>Odysseus, Paris, Priam, Zeus
>
>Level B: Eris, Oenone, Penelope, Thetis
>
>Level C: Hecuba, Peleus, Helen's baby daughter

Map Work:

>Level A: Aegean Sea, Black Sea, Greece, Sparta, Troy
>
>Level B: Ithaca, Olympus
>
>Level C: Ida

Comprehension Questions and Answers

Q1: Where did the golden apple come from?

>*Eris, upset at being left out of the party, threw it into the midst of the revelers.*

Q2: Who wanted the apple?

>*Hera, Athene and Aphrodite*

Q3: What happened to Paris when he was a baby? Why?

>*He was left in the wilderness to die because of a prophecy that said he would destroy Troy.*

Q4: What kind of a person is Paris?

>*Tall, strong, beautiful, fast, fickle, spoiled, irresistible, in love with beauty, etc.*

Q5: What did the goddesses ask Paris to do?

Paris was asked to decide to whom the golden apple

belonged.

Q6: What made Paris choose Aphrodite?

The promise of the most beautiful woman in the world.

Q7: Who was the most beautiful woman in the world? Who was
her husband?

Helen was the woman. Menelaus was her husband.

Q8: What did Paris and Helen do?

Helen left her husband to go live with Paris.

Suggested Lines of Discussion to Pursue

DQ1: How do the gods interact with mankind in this chapter?

The Greek gods grant wishes. They get angry with humans.

They put thoughts in people's heads. They also argue

among themselves and use Paris, a human, to settle

their argument.

DQ2: What do the Greeks believe about their gods?

The Greeks believe the gods are immortal. The gods are

depicted as fighting among themselves and as being at

parties with mortals. We also see that time is different for

them than it is for humans.

DQ3: How are the Greek gods different from the God of the Bible?

The Greek gods are many. Each represents a different aspect of nature (eg: gods of the sea, the earth, the harvest, etc.) or a different facet of the human experience (eg: love, strife, etc.). The God of the Bible is One God with three persons: the Father, the Son, and the Holy Spirit. He is the Creator of all things and rules all of them. Humans bear His likeness.

The Greek gods are sinful. They fight among themselves. They are jealous. They use others for their own ends. The God of the Bible is perfectly holy and righteous. Instead of using His power to manipulate humanity, He loves His creatures with a perfect love.

The Greek gods live in a physical location. They beget children. The God of the Bible is a spirit and, as the catechism says, does not have a body like men. He does not take wives from among humanity and breed with them like the Greek gods do. (With older students you could have a discussion about your church's view on Mary being with child by the Holy Spirit and what that means.)

DQ4: The story says Oenone is a "wood nymph". What is a nymph in Greek mythology?

In Greek mythology, a nymph is a minor goddess who is identified with and cares for some aspect of creation, such as trees (dryads) or rivers (naiads).

Chapter 2: Ship Gathering

Characters Introduced in this Chapter

>Level A: Achilles, Agamemnon
>
>Level B: Ajax, Calchas, Chiron, Diomedes, Hephaestus,
>
>>Patroclus
>
>Level C: Idomeneus, Lycomedes, Nestor

Map Work

>Level A: Crete
>
>Level B: Mycenae
>
>Level C: Argos, Aulis Harbor, Pylos, Pytho, Salamis,
>
>>Scyros, Thessaly, Thisbe, River Styx (not on map)

Comprehension Questions and Answers

Q1: Why is the league of Greeks setting out to attack Troy?

>*Paris ran away with Helen, Menelaus' wife. The Greek kings had alliances with Menelaus, so when he went to fight, they were obligated to fight with him.*

Q2: Who are Achilles' parents? What is unusual about his mother?

>*Peleus, his father, is a human, and Thetis, his mother, is a nymph.*

Q3: Why is Thetis afraid for Achilles?

>*When she dipped him in the river Styx, in order to give him immortality, she was holding him by the heel, and the supernatural water did not get on it. Through the back of*

his heel alone could Achilles be conquered.

Q4: How did Thetis try to keep Achilles out of the war?

> *Thetis dressed Achilles as a woman and sent him to live with the daughters of King Lycomedes.*

Q5: What trick did Odysseus play? Why?

> *Odysseus dressed as a trader and brought gifts to the daughters of King Lycomedes. The gift for Achilles was a sword, which he readily accepted, taking his place among the Greek forces.*

Suggested Lines of Discussion to Pursue

DQ1: Achilles' mother dipped him into the river Styx in order to grant him immortality. Do you think this was a moral act (a right thing to do)? Would you pursue immortality in this way if it were an option?

> *Answers to this question will vary. For Thetis, the act could be considered moral, since the story says that the gods instructed her to do it. For the Christian, obedience to God is a moral act, so it could follow that for Thetis, her obedience was moral according to the ancient Greeks' moral code. For Christians, this behavior would be forbidden as it would be sorcery. It is interesting, however, to think about the advantages and the drawbacks of being a human with bodily immortality.*

DQ2: The Greek kings went to fight with Menelaus because they had alliances with him. Is it always right to fight on behalf of a friend, just because you are friends?

> *Honoring a promise is a good thing. Loyalty to a friend is also a good thing. But what if a friend decides to do something dangerous or wrong? Should you defend his decision? Sometimes loving a friend means helping them in a way they don't like, such as telling someone in authority what dangerous or wrong thing the friend is planning to do.*

Chapter 3: Quarrel with the High King

<u>Characters Introduced in this Chapter</u>

> Level A: Apollo, Chryseis, Hector

> Level B: Briseis

> Level C: Chryseis' father, Protesilaus

<u>Comprehension Questions and Answers</u>

Q1: How long did the Greeks camp outside Troy?

> *9 years*

Q2: What were they doing during all that time?

> *Raiding smaller towns.*

Q3: Why did the Greeks believe that sickness came upon them?

> *They believed that Apollo was angry with them because*
>
> *Agamemnon had kidnapped Chryseis, who was the daughter*
>
> *of Apollo's priest.*

Q4: Whose side was Athene on? Aphrodite?

> *Athene was for the Greeks; Aphrodite was for the Trojans*

Q5: Why were Achilles and Agamemnon fighting?

> *Agamemnon said that if he had to give back Chryseis, then*
>
> *he would take Briseis from Achilles to take her place.*
>
> *Achilles was opposed to this idea. He liked Briseis.*

Q6: What did Achilles pray for?

> *Achilles prayed for a Trojan victory, as vengeance against*
>
> *Agamemnon for taking Briseis from him.*

Suggested Lines of Discussion to Pursue

Discussion Note: Homer's *Iliad* begins with this part of the story. The parts of *Black Ships Before Troy* that come before this were written in other ancient Greek texts.

DQ1: What do we learn about the Greeks' beliefs about their gods in this chapter? How do these things compare to the Christian's beliefs about God?

> *The Greeks believed that they had to keep the gods happy or suffering would come upon them. Christians also believe that God is displeased with sin and that he punishes sinners. But Christians also believe that God loves his creatures and intercedes for them in the person of Jesus Christ.*

> *The Greek gods had supernatural powers. We see Thetis in this chapter, making herself invisible to everyone but her son. We also find out that Thetis could hear Achilles from inside her crystal sea palaces. The God of the Bible also has supernatural powers. He can change the way he appears to humans (eg: the burning bush, the cloud that led Israel on the Exodus, etc.). He is all-seeing, all-knowing, all-powerful, and everywhere at once, unlike the Greek gods, who were limited.*

We see more instances of the gods fighting amongst themselves. Athene and Aphrodite took different sides in the war. Discuss how confusing it must have been to live in a world where the gods could be both for you and against you.

DQ2: Agamemnon sends cattle for a sacrifice to appease Apollo. How is this like Bible sacrifices? How is it different?

In the Old Testament, the Israelites made sacrifices to God, not unlike Agamemnon. But Agamemnon's sacrifices were meant only to quell the anger of Apollo. There was no more to the story than that. In the Bible, the sacrifices of the Old Testament were God's way of teaching His people that it was only through blood, the life-blood, that they could be saved. It was part of a larger story about salvation that would culminate in the shed blood of Jesus on the cross. Because of the sacrifices of the Old Testament, the people understood the seriousness of their sin as well as the earnest and loving intent of their Creator to restore their relationship with Him.

DQ3: Achilles prays for his own people to lose the war, in order to assuage his drive for vengeance against Agamemnon. Was this the right thing to do? Is there ever a circumstance where turning against your own people would be the right thing to do?

> *Achilles turns his personal vendetta into a request to the gods, with whom he had a voice in the person of his mother, Thetis. At best, this was a very immature thing to do, and at worst, a traitorous act against all of the Greeks. Is turning against your own people ever the right thing to do? Answers will vary, but stories could be brought up of people turning against their government or the tide of their culture when either of those entities was participating in or endorsing evil.*

DQ4: The Greeks, including Agamemnon, are fighting because Paris stole Menelaus' wife. Do you find it hypocritical that Agamemnon then steals Briseis from Achilles? Does it make a difference that she isn't his wife, but only his servant girl whom he loves?

> *There is irony here. Agamemnon sees Briseis as part of the spoils of war: an object to be owned. Paris saw Helen as an object as well, the prize for picking Aphrodite as the recipient of the golden apple. The war is being fought because Menelaus lost his wife, more to him than an object to be owned. The war is being lost because of the fight between*

Achilles and Agamemnon. To Achilles, Briseis is more than an object: he loves her. We don't see this in Black Ships Before Troy *as clearly as we see this in the* Iliad. *The Greeks only start winning again after Briseis is restored to Achilles, and the war ends with the return of Helen to Menelaus.*

Chapter 4: Single Combat

Characters Introduced in this Chapter

> Level B: Thersites

Comprehension Questions and Answers

Q1: What did Zeus give Agamemnon?

> *Zeus gave Agamemnon a false dream. Explain that the*
> *Greek gods lie when it suits their purposes.*

Q2: How were they going to end the conflict?

> *They were going to have a duel between Paris and Menelaus*
> *to decide who got Helen and her jewels.*

Q3: What does Aphrodite do in the duel?

> *Aphrodite made Paris' helmet come off so that he can*
> *escape. Then she gave him a cloak of invisibility.*

Q4: Who won the duel? Why?

> *Menelaus won the duel, because Paris disappeared.*

Q5: What is Helen's response when Paris shows up after the duel?

> *She wants to go back to Menelaus, her husband, because*
> *legally she belongs to him since he won the duel.*

Q6: What did Aphrodite do to Helen?

> *Aphrodite made Helen want to stay with Paris, even though*
> *she didn't want to in her own will.*

Q7: Why did Aphrodite want Helen to stay with Paris?

> *Aphrodite was the one who promised Helen to Paris. She*

thinks if Helen goes back to Menelaus she will look foolish in
the eyes of the other gods.

Suggested Lines of Discussion to Pursue

DQ1: Was Odysseus right to tell the army that it was shameful to leave after such a long siege? Or were the men right to want to go home?

> *It is virtuous to stand by a promise even when it is hard. One*
> *could argue that this was what the Greek army was doing in*
> *continuing the siege. It is also virtuous to be present with*
> *and care for your family. So the men could also be*
> *considered virtuous for wanting to go home. Discuss how*
> *difficult it is to make decisions when you are stuck between*
> *two moral options.*

DQ2: In the beginning of the chapter, Zeus gave Agamemnon a false dream. In the Bible, does God ever give people dreams? Are they ever false dreams?

> *In the Bible, God gives people dreams. An example is in*
> *Matthew 2, when God sends a dream to Joseph telling him*
> *to take Mary and Jesus to Egypt where they will be safe. In*
> *Daniel 7, Daniel is given a prophetic dream about coming*
> *kingdoms. God clearly uses dreams throughout the Bible.*
> *The Bible also speaks of false dreams, but these dreams are*
> *not from God. Deuteronomy 13 and Jeremiah 27 both*

counsel God's people not to listen to the dreamers of dreams, whose intent is to deceive and to cause the people of God to turn their backs on him. In John 14, Jesus says "I am the way, the truth and the life." The truth. God does not lie. That is the devil's work.

Chapter 5: The Women of Troy

Characters Introduced in this Chapter

>Level A: Hades

>Level B: Aeneas, Andromache, Machaon

>Level C: Astyanax, Pandarus, Sarpedon

Comprehension Questions and Answers

Q1: Why did the war keep going after the duel was over?

>*Athene put it in Pandarus' head to shoot Menelaus. This broke the truce.*

Q2: Who was winning the battle before the Trojan soothsayer came to Hector?

>*The Greeks.*

Q3: Why doesn't Hector want to make a sacrifice to the gods?

>*He is too dirty from battle to present himself in the presence of the gods.*

Q4: What is Paris doing during the battle? What is his excuse?

>*Paris is playing around with his weapons and armor like they are toys. He says he was too upset to go to battle because he knows it was his fault, so he is pausing to gather his strength.*

Q5: What is Helen's response to Paris' delay?

>*Helen thinks Paris cowardly for needing to be coaxed into battle.*

Q6: Why did Hector go to find his wife before returning to the battle?

He believed he was going to die and wanted to say goodbye.

Q7: What does Hector believe will happen to Troy? To Andromache?

Hector believes all his father's house will be destroyed and that Andromache and his baby son will become slaves.

Suggested Lines of Discussion to Pursue

DQ1: Hector does not want to make a sacrifice to the gods while he is still dirty from battle. What does this tell us about the Greek attitude toward their gods? Should Christians also have this attitude?

The Greek gods require cleanliness as a means to show respect. Christians ought to respect God. We ought to offer to God our best. But our God is merciful. The blood of Jesus covers our sins. It is acceptable and even desirable that we seek God while we are unclean, both literally and figuratively. As Christians we know that we cannot, in our own selves or with our own works, please God. The only cleanness of the soul is the cleansing work of the blood of Jesus.

DQ2: Helen disrespects Paris for cowardice because he doesn't want to go into battle. Is it always cowardly to avoid war?

> *Answers will vary depending on your personal views about war. Discuss those views. Talk about the difference between cowardice and pacifism. Just war theory says that there are legitimate reasons to go to war and that war should not be conducted in the absence of those reasons.*

Chapter 6: The High King's Embassy

Characters Introduced in this Chapter

> Level C: Phoenix

Comprehension Questions and Answers

Q1: Why did Athene decide to stop the fighting?

> *Too many Greeks were dying.*

Q2: Who is the "High King"?

> *Agamemnon.*

Q3: Which two men were selected for single combat?

> *Hector, the Trojan who issued the challenge, and Ajax, the tallest and strongest of the Greeks, who won the right to fight by lot.*

Q4: Who won the duel?

> *No one. They agreed to a friendly draw at the end of the day.*

Q5: Why were the Greeks unable to conquer the Trojans when the fighting began again?

> *Zeus intervened, sending lightning down to thwart them.*

Q6: What did Agamemnon want to do? Why?

> *Agamemnon wanted to go home because he believed that if Zeus was against him, there was no use in fighting.*

Q7: What alternate plan was suggested by Nestor?

> *Nestor advises them to get Achilles to join the fight again,*

because he knows the Trojans will be scared of him.

Q8: What was Achilles' reply to the request that the others make of him?

He says he doesn't trust Agamemnon. He will only fight if the Trojans attack him directly.

Suggested Lines of Discussion to Pursue

DQ1: After the duel, Hector and Ajax exchanged gifts, and it seems that both esteemed each other greatly. What does this tell us about the values that the ancient Greeks and Trojans held? Do you think this is a good way to think about the opposing side in a war?

Bravery was revered. Fighting was not a personal vendetta but was done for a cause larger than the individual. Those who fought bravely and well were respected, no matter which side they were on. Yet in battle, a warrior could kill an opponent freely without hatred or anger, and mourn his death with all his heart. It seems preposterous to us now that such respect and goodwill should endure among warring armies, but our values are different. In the modern Western world, a high value is placed upon life itself. For the ancient Greeks, it would seem, a higher value was placed upon valor, bravery, and victory.

DQ2: Phoenix urges Achilles to be a great enough man to let go of his anger when forgiveness has been asked and restitution paid. He says the anger was only appropriate while the injury remained. What does this tell us about how the Greeks viewed revenge?

> *The Greeks believed in justice. They lost respect for Achilles when he would not grant forgiveness when it was asked of him. Grudges were dishonorable.*

Chapter 7: The Horses of King Rhesus

Characters Introduced in this Chapter

> Level C: Dolon, King Rhesus of Thrace

Map Work

> Level C: Thrace

Comprehension Questions and Answers

Q1: What plan did Menelaus and the council instigate, in order to learn what the next day would hold?

> *They would send two men to spy on the Trojan camp in the*
> *night.*

Q2: Who will carry out Menelaus' plan?

> *Diomedes and Odysseus*

Q3: What plan did Hector begin at the same time? Who answered his request?

> *Hector decides to send a spy into the Greek camp to find out*
> *if the Greeks were keeping watch, or if they could be taken*
> *while sleeping. A foolish and ugly soldier named Dolon*
> *answered his request.*

Q4: What animal are Diomedes and Odysseus compared to? What about Dolon?

> *Diomedes and Odysseus are compared to lions; Dolon to a*
> *wolf.*

Q5: What happens to Dolon?

Diomedes kills him.

Q6: What did Odysseus and Diomedes do with the information they learned from Dolon?

Odysseus and Diomedes killed King Rhesus and his guards and stole their fine white horses.

Suggested Lines of Discussion to Pursue

DQ1: Was it fair for Diomedes to kill Dolon after Dolon had told him everything he wanted to know?

It could be argued that the Greeks were justified in killing Dolon because if they let him live, he would come spying again. This was defensible behavior because they were at war with his people. It could also be argued that Diomedes acted dishonorably because they could have found another way to keep Dolon from spying, such as taking him prisoner.

DQ2: Diomedes and Odysseus kill King Rhesus and his twelve companions while they are sleeping soundly. Did this bother you? Is there a moral difference between killing during a battle and killing sleeping men during a raid on the enemy camp?

Answers will vary. It could be argued that the only fair war-

time killing would be killing during a battle. It could also be argued that the killings were fair because King Rhesus and his companions were not innocent civilians but warriors come for the specific purpose of killing the Greeks. In killing King Rhesus the Greeks were preventing their own deaths.

Chapter 8: Red Rain

Characters Introduced in this Chapter

> Level B: Pan

> Level C: Eurypolus, Hecamede

Comprehension Questions and Answers

Q1: What strange phenomenon happens? Who does it happen to? Why?

> *Red rain begins to fall over the Greek camp. Zeus sent it to them.*

Q2: Why are shepherds quiet at noon?

> *For fear of rousing Pan.*

Q3: What happened to Agamemnon in the battle?

> *Agamemnon is wounded in the arm and has to go back to the ships to be treated.*

Q4: What happened to Diomedes in the battle? Odysseus?

> *Diomedes is speared through the foot; Odysseus is wounded between the ribs.*

Q5: Why are the Greeks particularly worried when Machaon is wounded?

> *Machaon is the one among them who knows how to treat battle injuries. They will be in bad shape without a doctor.*

Q6: Why did Achilles send Patroclus to Nestor?

> *To find out how Machaon is doing.*

Q7: What idea does Nestor give Patroclus?

Nestor suggests that Patroclus disguise himself as Achilles and go into battle.

Suggested Lines of Discussion to Pursue

DQ1: Who is Pan and why would the shepherds fear rousing him?

Pan was the god of hunters and of shepherds and their flocks. He slept at noon and became very angry if he were awakened. Pan had pointed ears, a beard, horns, and the legs and hooves of a goat.

DQ2: Should Achilles have joined the Greeks in fighting, despite his grudge against Agamemnon?

Achilles grudge was against Agamemnon alone, not against the other Greeks and not against Menelaus. It was the wrong done to Menelaus that the Greeks had come to avenge. In refusing to fight he forgets the cause of the war. Contrariwise, Agamemnon is the High King and the one in charge of the Greek forces. And Agamemnon did wrong Achilles. It can be argued that Achilles was justified in refusing to fight under such a leader, knowing that Agamemnon had such disrespect for him.

Chapter 9: Battle for the Ships

Characters Introduced in this Chapter

Level A: Poseidon

Level C: Asios, Glaucus, Helenus

Map Work

Level C: Xanthus River

Comprehension Questions and Answers

Q1: In the opening scene of this chapter, what are the Trojans trying to do?

The Trojans are trying to cross the moat and the wall into the Greek camp.

Q2: Why do the Trojans think that Zeus is against them? How does Hector refute this?

An eagle, the bird of Zeus, dropped a live, blood-red snake in their midst. They regarded this as an evil omen. Hector refutes this by telling them that the best omen was to fight for their country.

Q3: What assistance does Zeus give the Trojans?

Zeus allows Hector to lift an impossibly heavy stone and hurl it at the Greek gates, breaking them.

Q4: What does Zeus do after he helps the Trojans?

Zeus abandons them. He has other things to think about.

Q5: What god intervenes next? Over what natural things does he rule? What does he do?

> *Poseidon, lord of the ocean and earthquakes, came up on the beach with a host of monsters. He gives a feeling of encouragement to the Greeks.*

Q6: Who is injured in the Greek charge?

> *Hector.*

Q7: What does Zeus do when he sees the injured man?

> *Zeus sends Apollo to help Hector.*

Q8: What does the revived Hector do?

> *Hector leads a fierce charge against the Greeks, driving them back to their ships and sets half of the Greek fleet on fire.*

Suggested Lines of Discussion to Pursue

DQ1: Do the Trojans heed the evil omen of the red snake and stop fighting? Why? What does this tell you about what they think about their gods?

> *When Hector advises them that the best omen is to fight for their country, they listen to him and keep fighting. This tells us that the people seem to regard the authority of Zeus and the authority of Hector as more similar than we would regard man's authority versus God's. This is the second time in the book that an omen was dismissed by a king, at which time the people followed the king instead of the god.*

DQ2: What do we learn about the Greek gods in this chapter? Contrast these things with the characteristics of the God of the Bible.

The Greek gods fight among themselves and take sides. There is no all-powerful god among them, for Zeus has no power to conquer his brother, Poseidon, who is his equal. We also learn that they are able to heal desperate injuries.

The God of the Bible is all-powerful. Too often, Satan is depicted as being the antithesis of God: an opposite and an equal. This is not the case. Satan is a fallen angel, and is not the 'evil god' set in opposition to the 'good God'. The God of the Bible is able to heal desperate injuries, just as Apollo was able to breathe fresh life into Hector.

Chapter 10: The Armor of Achilles

Characters Introduced in this Chapter

Level B: Automedon, the West Wind

Level C: Balius, Death, Pedasus, Sleep, Xanthus

Comprehension Questions and Answers

Q1: Why does Achilles taunt Patroclus?

Patroclus was crying "like a little girl" because of the misfortune of the Greeks.

Q2: Why is Achilles grieved?

He has vowed not to join the fight until the Trojans attacked him directly. He wants to join the fight, but he can't because of his vow.

Q3: What is unusual about the two horses, Xanthus and Balius?

They had been fathered by the West Wind and were immortal. The story contrasts them with Pedasus, the "mortal horse".

Q4: What does Patroclus do?

Wearing the armor of Achilles, he leads the Myrmidons against the Trojans.

Q5: Who does Achilles pray to? What is his prayer?

Achilles prays to Zeus. He requests that Zeus would send glory and strength of heart to Patroclus, and that Patroclus and the men would return unharmed.

Q6: What happens to Sarpedon?

Sarpedon is killed. The Greeks steal his armor. Sarpedon was the son of a mortal woman and Zeus. Zeus orders Sleep and Death to carry the body of Sarpedon away for burial, so that he disappears from the battlefield.

Q7: Why didn't Patroclus return to Achilles right away as he promised?

Zeus, angry over the death of his son, Sarpedon, sends a rage into Patroclus so that he continues to fight like a crazy man.

Q8: What happens to Patroclus? What does he prophesy?

Hector kills Patroclus. Just before he dies, he predicts that Hector will be slain in the same spot, by Achilles.

Q9: Who wants the body of Patroclus? Why?

The Greeks want to take him with them for honorable burial. The Trojans want his body so they can fling it to the dogs in the city.

Q10: Who remains unmoving beside the body of Patroclus? What happens to them?

The two immortal horses, Xanthus and Balius, remain with Patroclus. Zeus puts a fiery spirit within them so that they return to the battle, pulling Automedon's chariot.

Q11: Who is winning the battle at the end of this chapter?

The Trojans.

Suggested Lines of Discussion to Pursue

DQ1: Achilles was grieved because his vow prevented him from fighting. What does Achilles' grief demonstrate about the values of the Greeks? Is it ever right to break a vow?

> *The Greeks place a high value on faithfulness. Achilles has sworn not to fight until the Trojans set fire to his own ships, and he will not break his vow, even though he wishes to.*
>
> *The Bible places a high value on keeping your word. But it also places a high value on righteousness. An unrighteous vow should be broken. Discuss examples of unrighteous vows from the Bible or from your current life. (For example, a child vows not to obey their parents until he gets his own way...)*

DQ2: What does the story of the death of Sarpedon tell us about the gods?

> *The Greek gods can procreate with humans. Sarpedon was the son of Zeus and a mortal woman. Also, we see that Zeus keeps track of his mortal offspring. Sleep and Death are regarded as gods themselves, and not just as states of being.*

Chapter 11: Vengeance for Patroclus

Characters Introduced in this Chapter

> Level C: Antilochus

Comprehension Questions and Answers

Q1: What does Antilochus tell Achilles?

> *Antilochus tells Achilles that Patroclus is dead and that the armies are fighting for his body. Hector, he says, has Achilles' armor.*

Q2: Why does Thetis tell Achilles not to go into battle yet? What is she going to do?

> *Achilles does not have any armor. Thetis is going to visit the god Hephaestus in his forge and bring Achilles new armor.*

Q3: Who ended up with the body of Patroclus? How did this come about?

> *Achilles and the Greeks got Patroclus' body. The Trojans abandoned it in terror when they saw Achilles shouting at them from the highest rampart.*

Q4: Describe or draw the armor Hephaestus makes for Achilles.

> *Breastplate and shin guards made of bronze, silver, tin, and gold. A tall, crested helmet of red gold. A shield inlaid with precious metals showing pictures of cities, seas, and battles, a lion hunt, fields ripe with corn, vineyards full of grapes, and men and women dancing to the voice of flutes.*

Q5: Why does Odysseus delay Achilles' return to battle?

> *The rules of honor say that Achilles must make peace with Agamemnon before he can return to the fight on the same side as him.*

Q6: Who gives Achilles a prophecy? What is that prophecy?

> *Xanthus, the horse, given speech by the goddess Hera, prophesies that Achilles' death is near.*

Q7: What is Hector's fate? What does he request?

> *He dies after Achilles drives a sword through his neck. He asks Achilles to return his body to his father and offers him gold to do it. Achilles refuses.*

Q8: What does Achilles do with Hector's body?

> *Drags it behind his chariot in the dust.*

Suggested Lines of Discussion to Pursue

DQ1: Do some research to learn more about the shield of Achilles. It is said to represent a microcosm of the Iliad itself. Online resources are plentiful.

DQ2: What do we learn about the Greeks' values because of Odysseus' decision to have Achilles make peace with Agamemnon before returning to battle?

> *The Greeks have a strict code of honor, even though it is different from our own. They must make sacrifices to the*

gods, with "all due ceremonies". Achilles must demonstrate his forgiveness for Agamemnon by receiving the gifts he previously offered to him in restitution.

DQ3: The goddess Hera gives a prophecy through the horse Xanthus that Achilles' death is near. What does this tell us about the Greek gods? Does the God of the Bible share these qualities?

The Greek gods knew in advance what was going to happen. Also, they can perform miracles, like making a horse talk. In the Bible, God can and does perform miracles, including making a donkey talk (Numbers 22). The God of the Bible knows what is going to happen in advance. He is outside time.

DQ4: Does Achilles do right by showing no mercy to Hector in the end? By refusing to assure him that he will return his body to his father as he is dying?

Achilles is clearly wrong in the way he treats Hector's body. He allowed his temper to control him. Killing Hector was an act of war, and Hector would have expected no less from a worthy opponent. But even the gods were angry with Achilles for the disrespect he showed in abusing the body of Hector and refusing to return the corpse to the Trojans.

DQ5: In chapter 3, we see Achilles praying for the Greeks to lose the war. Does Achilles bear some responsibility for the death of Patroclus?

The text indicates that Zeus exacts vengeance on Patroclus because he killed Sarpedon. Had Zeus not put a fierce battle-rage into Patroclus, he would have returned to Achilles and not died. Achilles does feel incredible grief over the death of his best friend, but it does not seem he associates it with his prayer. Still, it seems possible that Zeus' actions in the battle were part of a larger plan to help the Trojans win.

Chapter 12: Funeral Games

Characters Introduced in this Chapter

> Level C: Epeius, Eumelus, Euryalus, Meriones

Comprehension Questions and Answers

Q1: Why is Andromache sad?

> *Her husband, Hector is dead.*

Q2: Why does Andromache believe that Hector will not proceed to the next life in Hades?

> *Lacking a proper burial, he would have to wander, ghostlike, in the borderlands between the living and the dead.*

Q3: What vision does Achilles have?

> *The ghost of Patroclus comes to Achilles, asking for burial, and to greet him one last time before he is gone forever.*

Q4: Describe the ceremonies that were given to usher Patroclus into the next world.

> *They burned Patroclus' body with locks of hair from all, slain cattle, slain Trojans, four horses and two of Achilles' favorite dogs. After that they put Patroclus' ashes into a golden cup and put the cup into a stone vault. This was followed by chariot races, boxing, wrestling, a foot race, and a spear fight. After that there was a feast.*

Q5: What does Achilles do as a result of his violent grief?

> *Behind his chariot, he drags the body of Hector three times around Patroclus' grave. He does this for 12 nights.*

Q6: What do the gods think about this?

> *They are angry with Achilles and vow to make it stop. Apollo protects Hector's body from more harm.*

Suggested Lines of Discussion to Pursue

DQ1: Andromache believes that without a proper burial, the dead have to wander in the borderlands between the living and the dead. What does this tell us about the Greek beliefs about the gods and the afterlife? Compare this to the Christian beliefs about life after death.

> *Perhaps this indicates that the Greek gods lack mercy. Hector was a revered man, but for lack of something happening after his life was over, and over which he had no control, he could be denied admission to the land of the dead.*
>
> *The Bible offers several viewing points for life after death. To the thief on the cross, Jesus proclaims, "Today you will be with me in paradise." (Luke 23:43). In I Thessalonians 4, the text refers to the dead as those who have fallen asleep. And in Luke 16 the Bible tells of a dead man who was waiting in Abraham's bosom. We know from the Bible that man's final*

destination is eternal life with Jesus, and that God will recreate the heavens and the earth as a dwelling place for His people and His kingdom. But is there a time of waiting or sleeping that precedes the arrival in the final kingdom? Does the soul immediately join God but the body has to wait for a bodily resurrection? Discuss.

DQ2: What does Achilles' vision of Patroclus tell us about the Greeks' beliefs?

Patroclus says that the other ghosts won't let him join them unless he has a proper burial. This seems to imply that it is not just the gods who do the admissions to Hades, but the spirits within. He also tells us that once someone goes to Hades, he cannot return.

DQ3: Apollo protects Hector's body from further harm by Achilles. What does this tell us about the Greek gods?

The Greek gods are willing to intervene in human affairs in order to preserve justice and honor. More often we see them intervening in human affairs for their own motives. This seems more altruistic than the behavior we have seen thus far.

Chapter 13: Ransom for Hector

<u>Characters Introduced in this Chapter</u>

>Level A: Hermes

>Level B: Iris

>Level C: Deiphobos

<u>Comprehension Questions and Answers</u>

Q1: How did the gods persuade Achilles to stop abusing the body of Hector?

>*They sent his mother, Thetis, to persuade him.*

Q2: What message did Iris take to Priam?

>*Iris told Priam that if offered a ransom, Achilles would give him Hector's body.*

Q3: What help did Hermes give to Priam?

>*He caused the Greeks to fall asleep so that no one saw Priam coming into the Greek camp.*

Q4: What are some of Hector's good qualities that the mourners enumerate?

>*Hecuba notes that he was beloved by the gods. Helen says that he was always kind and gentle with her, even when others had harsh words.*

Q5: How was the funeral of Hector different from the funeral of Patroclus?

>*He was burned without animals or human sacrifices. There*

were no funeral games.

Suggested Lines of Discussion to Pursue

DQ1: Of the heroes in the book, Odysseus, Achilles, and Hector, who is your favorite? Why?

> *Answers will vary.*

DQ2: Did Achilles change from the spoiled, immature boy into a gracious and mature man with his new willingness to return Hector's body to Priam? Or was he only trying to please his mother and the gods, whom he feared in their anger toward him?

> *When we first see Achilles in the book, he is enraged because Agamemnon stole Briseis from him. As soon as the rift between Achilles and Agamemnon is patched, Achilles turns his rage on Hector, because of his extreme grief over the death of Patroclus. It might be argued that Achilles does not change at all. He begins as a man controlled by his passions and ends the same way. First he is driven by rage against Agamemnon and then Hector. And then he is driven by grief to avenge Patroclus, and later he is able to turn that grief toward his own father as Priam begs for the body of Hector.*

Discussion Note: Homer's *Iliad* ends here, with the return of Hector's body and before the death of Achilles. The story of the Trojan horse is found in Virgil's *Aeneid*. The *Aeneid* is the story of the Trojan Aeneas and how he founded Rome.

Chapter 14: The Luck of Troy

Characters Introduced in this Chapter

> Level B: Memnon, Penthesilea

> Level C: Thrasymedes, a queen of Egypt, the king of Delos

Map Work

> Level C: Delos

Comprehension Questions and Answers

Q1: Why is the war at a standstill?

> *The Greeks are worn out. The Trojans are afraid to venture forth against them because their leader is dead. They are also waiting for reinforcements.*

Q2: What was the Palladium?

> *A black stone shaped like Athene's shield. It was called the "Luck of Troy". The Trojans believed that as long as it was there, Athene would keep their enemies out of the city.*

Q3: What plan does Odysseus devise?

> *Odysseus decide to steal the Palladium.*

Q4: Why did the Greeks kick the beggar out of their camp?

> *He was generally obnoxious and topped it all off by stealing a golden cup from Nestor.*

Q5: How did the beggar get Helen to take care of him?

> *He promised to tell her of her family back in Greece.*

Q6: Who was the beggar?

Odysseus.

Q7: How did Odysseus manage to steal the Palladium?

He drugged the priestess on guard, substituted a clay model
for the real Palladium, and crept away.

Suggested Lines of Discussion to Pursue

DQ1: Does Odysseus believe that the power of Athene rests with
the Palladium? Why do you think that?

It seems not. He wants to steal it because he knows that the
Trojans will lose heart and then lose the war, not because he
thinks it will sway Athene to his side or take real power away
from Troy.

DQ2: Did you know all along that the beggar was Odysseus? What
clues did you have?

Answers will vary. Possible clues include the fact that the
book doesn't say who the beggar is, that Odysseus was away
when the beggar appeared. Also, we know that Odysseus
has a plan, and leaving the battle for a month seems out of
character for him.

DQ3: Why do you think that Odysseus chose to reveal himself to Helen, when he might has stayed disguised as a beggar?

>*Answers will vary. Perhaps he feared she might recognize him despite the disguise. Maybe he wanted to win her to his side or to reassure Helen, his old friend, that he would do everything in his power to spare her life.*

Chapter 15: Warrior Women

Characters Introduced in this Chapter

>Level A: Ares

>Level C: Hippolyta

Map Work

>Level C: River Thermodon

Comprehension Questions and Answers

Q1: Who are the Amazons?

>*The Amazons are a band of warrior women.*

Q2: Why did Penthesilea decide to become a warrior?

>*Full of grief after she accidentally killed her sister,*
>
>*Penthesilea decided she wanted to die, and to do it*
>
>*gloriously and in battle.*

Q3: What happened to the Amazons?

>*They were killed by the Greeks.*

Suggested Lines of Discussion to Pursue

DQ1: Did the Greeks and the Trojans treat the women soldiers differently than they treated men soldiers?

>*In the book it seems not. They fought the women with as*
>
>*much furor as that with which they fought the men. After*
>
>*they were dead, though, it seems they took time to address*
>
>*their femininity. They did not take their armor but sent the*
>
>*bodies back to Troy with honor.*

DQ2: Is it appropriate for woman to fight in wars?

> *The general pattern of scripture shows that it is the men who fight the wars, and the women tend the home and care for the children. There are examples in the Bible, however of women taking a role in battle, such as Deborah and Jael. While they are the exception and not the rule, they are praised for their leadership and courage, and not condemned for acting against type.*

DQ3: Was the Amazon River named after the Amazon women, or were the women named after the river?

> *A Spanish explorer, Francisco de Orellana, named the river "Amazon" after the tribe of Amazon women in Greek mythology. He had observed tribal women fighting alongside the men in battle in that region and it reminded him of the Amazons in the* Iliad.

Chapter 16: The Death of Achilles

Characters Introduced in this Chapter

Level A: Dionysus

Level C: Polydamas

Comprehension Questions and Answers

Q1: Why were the Trojans hiding out inside the walls of Troy?

They were waiting for King Memnon and the Ethiopians to join them in battle.

Q2: What suggestion does Polydamas make?

Polydamas suggests that they just give Helen back, along with double the amount of jewels she came with.

Q3: Why does Polydamas' suggestion make Paris angry?

He wants to keep Helen, and cares little for what happens to Troy.

Q4: Who does Memnon kill first?

Antilochus.

Q5: Who kills Memnon?

Achilles.

Q6: What prevented the Greeks from taking Troy that day?

Paris' arrow, guided by Apollo, finds its mark in Achilles' heel, killing him.

Q7: What do they do with Achilles ashes?

They mingle Achilles' ashes in the golden cup with the ashes of Patroclus.

Q8: What becomes of Achilles' armor?

> *Achilles' mother, Thetis, tells them that it shall belong to the*
> *best and bravest of the two Greek warriors who rescued*
> *Achilles' body: Odysseus or Ajax. That the competition*
> *might not divide the Greeks, they decide to let the Trojan*
> *prisoners decide who gets the armor. Odysseus gets it.*

Q9: Why did the Trojan prisoners pick Odysseus?

> *The god Dionysus, a mischief-maker, made it sound like Ajax*
> *was drunk when he spoke on his own behalf.*

Q10: What becomes of Ajax?

> *The madness with which Dionysus afflicted him drove him in*
> *a drunken rage. He killed a bunch of sheep and then,*
> *waking from the madness, he killed himself rather than*
> *endure disgrace.*

Suggested Lines of Discussion to Pursue

DQ1: What do we learn about the Greek gods from the example of
Dionysus?

> *It would seem in this instance, that it was Ajax who was the*
> *nobler, rather than Dionysus, despite his divine status.*
> *Dionysus drove Ajax insane for his own amusement. Ajax*
> *took responsibility for his own insanity and did away with*
> *himself. We can conclude that sometimes the gods are*

selfish and have little regard for the virtue of particular men.

DQ2: Is it better to be dead or to be in disgrace? Why?

>*It depends on whether you value your life more or your reputation more. A reputation can be restored, however, and life cannot be. But a life sacrificed for Christ is never wasted. Life is not the most important thing: God and His kingdom and the souls of our neighbors are appropriate reasons for a person to give his life. But personal glory or reputation is not in that category.*

DQ3: Was it annoying that the title of the chapter was a spoiler, "The Death of Achilles"?

>*Answers will vary. If it had been up to me, I might have titled the chapter "The Downfall of Achilles" or something more ambiguous.*

DQ4: Achilles dies in the midst of a great battle, but he dies from an arrow shot from above. Paris is not fighting in the midst of the warriors, but it shooting arrows from the gate-tower. Is this characteristic of Paris? How?

>*Throughout the book Paris has proven himself a coward. He avoids battle as often as he can. It is completely characteristic of Paris that even in his moment of glory, the killing of the great hero Achilles, that he is withdrawn and aloof from the heat of the fight.*

Chapter 17: Poisoned Arrow

Characters Introduced in this Chapter

>   Level A: Heracles

>   Level B: the Fates, Philoctetes

Map Work

>   Level C: Lemnos

Comprehension Questions and Answers

Q1: What does the soothsayer Calchas advise the Greeks to do?

>   *Calchas tells the Greeks that they will not take Troy without*
>   *the help of Philoctetes, an archer the Greeks had abandoned*
>   *on the island of Lemnos.*

Q2: Who is Philoctetes?

>   *Philoctetes had been left by the Greeks on Lemnos ten years*
>   *before. He had battled a dragon, and though he killed it, he*
>   *received an agonizing, stinking wound that would not heal.*
>   *Ten years later he is still in agony.*

Q3: What power does Philoctetes possess that will enable him to help them?

>   *His wound gives off a foul poison. By dipping his arrows in*
>   *the poison, he is able to kill with a single shot.*

Q4: Who does Philoctetes shoot?

>   *Paris.*

Q5: Who does Paris flee to for comfort? What excuse does he give her?

> *Paris flees to his first love, Oenone. He tells her that he could not help loving Helen, that it was the Fates that made him a slave to his love for her.*

Q6: How does she respond to his pleas?

> *Oenone first tells Paris that he has made his choice: he ought to go back to Helen, for he had finished with her ten years ago. Then she relents and goes after him, but he is already dead. She throws herself on the funeral pyre and dies with Paris.*

Suggested Lines of Discussion to Pursue

DQ1: Philoctetes was abandoned by the Greeks, and then rescued because they wanted to use him. What do you think he is feeling now?

> *Answers will vary, but may include the ideas that he is angry at being left behind and then used, or grateful for his eventual rescue.*

DQ2: Do the Greeks believe they are responsible for their actions when the gods have intervened? Contrast Ajax with Paris.

> *Dionysus made Ajax go mad. In his rage, Ajax killed many sheep. Upon waking he cannot live with the disgrace and kills himself. Clearly he feels that he himself is responsible*

for his actions, even under the shadow of divinely-inspired madness. Paris, however, pleads that he was not to blame in the choice of Helen and whines for Oenone to forgive him and love him again.

DQ3: Oenone first rejects Paris' pleas for help. Paris had abandoned her for another woman ten years earlier and she felt she owed him nothing. Then, after he has died, she chooses to die with him for the sake of their love. What do you think about Oenone's decisions? Was dying with Paris a beautiful expression of love or a foolish waste of a life?

Answers will vary. Maybe Oenone, knowing the manipulative nature of the gods, could have seen that Paris might have been duped into loving Helen. She could have forgiven him. Or perhaps she thought ten years was an inexcusable amount of time. The gods may have pushed him toward Helen, but they did not hold him at her side for ten years. His own love did that. Either way, it is odd that she changes her mind and chooses to die rather than live without Paris. She had been living without Paris for ten years.

Chapter 18: The Wooden Horse

Characters Introduced in this Chapter

>Level A: Cassandra

>Level B: Laocoön, Sinon

>Level C: Palamedes, Laocoön's sons

Map Work

>Level C: Tenedos

Comprehension Questions and Answers

Q1: What recommendation does Calchas give the Greeks?

>*Calchas tells them that since they have failed to conquer Troy by strength, that it remains to them to try cunning.*

Q2: Where does Odysseus get his good idea?

>*Athena plants the idea of the Trojan horse in his mind.*

Q3: What story was to be told to the Trojans to explain the presence of a giant horse?

>*The Trojans were to be told that the horse was left by the Greeks as a gift to Athene. They were to be told that the Greeks were afraid that they had offended Athene by the theft of the Luck of Troy.*

Q4: How many men could fit in the belly of the horse?

>*A score of men could fit in the belly of the horse (20).*

Q5: Who warns the Trojans against the horse? Why don't they heed the warning?

Laocoön, high priest of Poseidon, warns them that the horse is a danger. Then they find Sinon, listen to his story and believe him.

Q6: What did the sea serpents do? What did the Trojans infer from that?

The sea serpents crushed Laocoön and his sons. Then they disappeared behind the feet of the statue of Athene. The Trojans believed it was a judgment of Athene against Laocoön for speaking against the horse.

Q7: Besides Laocoön, who warns the Trojans against the horse?

Cassandra, the old king's daughter, warns the Trojans that the horse will be the death of Troy.

Suggested Lines of Discussion to Pursue

DQ1: Were the Trojans dumb to take the horse into the city? How did their belief in the gods affect that decision?

The Trojans had good reason to believe the horse was a legitimate gift. The Greek ships were gone. Sinon's story made sense. Laocoön and Cassandra prophesied that the horse would bring destruction to Troy, even going so far as to offer evidence that the horse was hollow. The Trojans may have opted for Laocoön's interpretation of the horse, but when the sea monsters came up and crushed Laocoön and then disappeared in Athene's temple, they interpreted

that to mean that Athene was, indeed, angry, just as Sinon

had said. If they hadn't been led by their beliefs about the

gods, they might have seen through the ruse.

DQ2: Why didn't the Greeks return the Luck of Troy along with the gift of the horse? After all, their contention was that the horse was an offering to Athene to appease her wrath over the theft of the Luck of Troy. Wouldn't that have made Sinon's story more believable?

The Greeks believed that the Luck of Troy gave them an

advantage over the Trojans, one they didn't want to lose.

Chapter 19: The Fall of Troy

<u>Comprehension Questions and Answers</u>

Q1: What sign did the Greeks on the ships send to Sinon? What sign did Sinon give those inside the horse?

> *The Greeks on the ship signaled to Sinon with red fire. Sinon signaled to those inside the horse by imitating the cry of a shorebird.*

Q2: What happened to Priam? To the queen and princesses?

> *A young warrior killed Priam. The queen and princesses were taken captive.*

Q3: What request does Odysseus make of Menelaus? Why?

> *Odysseus requests that Menelaus spare Helen's life, just as Helen had saved his life when he stole the Luck of Troy.*

Q4: What happens to Helen in the end?

> *Helen is led home, not in chains like the other women, but as a queen.*

<u>Suggested Lines of Discussion to Pursue</u>

DQ1: What does this chapter tell us about the value the Greeks placed on keeping promises?

> *Odysseus made a promise to Helen, to save her life if he could. Menelaus promised a gift of his choice to Odysseus. Both were fully bound by their promises and fulfilled them. They are held up as noble for fulfilling their word.*

Extra Discussion Questions

DQ1: How is Paris' end in his beginning?

> *Offered wisdom, power & wealth, or a beautiful woman, he*
> *chooses the woman. His choices were dishonorable*
> *throughout the whole epic. He shows himself to be selfish*
> *and cowardly and irresponsible. He kills from afar and is*
> *himself killed by a poisoned arrow from afar. The Greeks*
> *believed that poisoning an arrow was not a fair practice.*

DQ2: Would the story have played out differently if Paris had chosen Athene (wisdom) or Hera (power) as the recipient of the apple?

> *Speculative. Answers will vary. Have fun with this discussion.*
> *Talk about alternate paths for the story. Write your own*
> *version(s) if you are so inclined.*

DQ3: The gods influence the story from beginning to end. Is it fair to hold the characters responsible for their actions?

> *We see that the Greeks believed it was fair. Contrast Paris'*
> *blame of the gods for his love for Helen in his whiny apology*
> *to Oenone with the other characters. Ajax kills himself*
> *rather than endure personal disgrace because of a madness*
> *that was not his fault. Odysseus is known for his cunning,*
> *but it tells us clearly that his cunning was given him by*
> *Athene. Achilles could have blamed his mother for the*

vulnerability in his heel, but he does not.

How do we view justice in light of our own inevitable sinfulness? Is God just to blame us? Read Romans 9: 19-21. God holds us responsible for our sin. His blame is just. It is His mercy that is unjust. (also Proverbs 16:1, 9 & 33; Romans 8:28 & Ephesians 1:11)

DQ4: Who was the most righteous character in this book? Why? Who was the most villainous? Why?

Answers will vary. Bring up the gods as well as the humans. The war began because of the actions of the gods and it was carried out by humans.

DQ5: Discuss the flow of Achilles' life. Was he a righteous man or an unrighteous one?

Achilles comes into the story in a big way when Agamemnon decides to appropriate his concubine, Briseis, to himself. In anger, Achilles refuses to fight with the Greeks anymore. He only comes back to fight after his friend, Patroclus, fights in his place and dies. Then Achilles goes into battle and kills Hector, but does great dishonor to his body. Discuss Achilles' choices with the student(s) as well as the nature of true righteousness.

DQ6: Which side represents the "good guys" in this story? Was this a just war? How do we define a just war?

>*The Greeks were presented as protagonist in this story. Because of the injustice done to Menelaus when Paris took Helen, the Greeks did have a valid complaint. However, there were noble people and fools on both sides. Discuss the idea of just war and how we define war as just today.*

DQ7: How did anger lead the Greeks into destruction? How do we see anger in our culture now (eg: the internet!) and how is it affecting us as a people?

>*Menelaus was angry with Paris (and Troy). Achilles was angry with Agamemnon. The gods get angry with each other and with humanity. The war began because of the anger sown by Eris, the goddess of strife. We see anger all around us. People are angry when others hurt them. People are angry when others disagree with them. Look at the internet. People are full of anger and hate and it spews out continually. Have a discussion about how to be a peacemaker and about how to handle feelings of anger. Talk about the difference between righteous anger and sinful anger.*

DQ8: How does our sin affect others? Consider Achilles in his anger refusing to fight.

> *Talk about how one person's actions can affect everyone around them. Give the students examples you have seen in their real lives.*

DQ9: Given the choice, would you choose a short life with glory, like Achilles and Hector, or a long life with no glory, like all the Greeks who never got into an epic tale?

> *Answers will vary.*

DQ10: Did you enjoy this book? Why or why not?

> *Answers will vary.*

Index of characters

Character	Chapter	Type	Level	Description
Achilles	2	demigod	A	Greek warrior. Son of Thetis, who gave him near total immortality. Refused to fight because of a disagreement with Agamemnon. Died avenging Patroclus' death.
Aeneas	5	man	B	A Trojan warrior.
Agamemnon	2	man	A	High King of the Greeks. Menelaus' brother.
Ajax	2	man	B	Greek warrior. Lord of Salamis.
Andromache	5	woman	B	Hector's wife
Antilochus	11	man	C	Greek warrior. Nestor's son.
Aphrodite	1	goddess	A	Goddess of beauty. Sided with the Trojans.
Apollo	3	god	A	The sun god.
Ares	15	god	A	God of war.
Asios	9	man	C	Most headstrong Trojan warrior.
Astyanax	5	man	C	Hector's son.
Athene	1	goddess	A	Goddess of wisdom. Sided with the Greeks.
Automedon	10	man	B	Achilles' charioteer.
Balius	10	horse	C	Immortal horse belonging to Achilles. Fathered by the West Wind.
Briseis	3	woman	B	Woman give to Achilles and subsequently taken by Agamemnon.
Calchas	2	man	B	Agamemnon's chief soothsayer.

Character	Chapter	Type	Level	Description
Cassandra	18	woman	A	Trojan priestess who prophesied doom for Troy. Daughter of Priam and Hecuba.
Chiron	2	centaur	B	Centaur. Greatest healer of all time.
Chryseis	3	woman	A	Maiden captured by Agamemnon thus inciting the anger of Apollo.
Chryseis' Father	3	man	C	His name was Chryses. Priest of Apollo.
Death	10	god	C	The personification of death. Named Than-atos (not in the text).
Deiphobos	13	man	C	Son of Priam and Hecuba. Takes Helen in after Paris' death.
Diomedes	2	man	B	King of Argos. Called Diomedes of the Loud War Cry. Greek warrior.
Dionysus	16	god	A	Greek god of wine. A mischief-maker.
Dolon	7	man	C	Foolish, ugly Trojan who loves horses. Killed while spying on the Greeks.
Epeius	12	man	C	Large Greek man. A boxer. Builder of the Trojan horse.
Eris	1	goddess	B	Goddess of discord. Threw the golden apple that started the Trojan war.
Eumelus	12	man	C	Greek warrior.
Euryalus	12	man	C	Greek warrior. A leader of the men from Argos.

Character	Chapter	Type	Level	Description
Eurypolus	8	man	C	Greek warrior.
Fates	17	other	B	Goddesses that decide the quality and length of everyone's lives. The Greek name for them was the Moirai.
Glaucus	9	man	C	Trojan warrior.
Hades	5	god	A	Greek god of the underworld.
Hecamede	8	woman	C	Servant woman of Nestor.
Hector	3	man	A	Prince of Troy. Son of Priam and Hecuba. Dies in the Trojan war and his body is dishonored. Called Tamer of Horses.
Hecuba	1	woman	C	Priam's wife. Queen of Troy. Mother of Paris and Hector.
Helen	1	woman	A	Wife of Menelaus. Most beautiful woman in the world. Stolen away by Paris. Called Helen of the Fair Cheeks.
Helen's baby	1	woman	C	Baby daughter of Helen and Menelaus. Named Hermione.
Helenus	9	man	C	Trojan warrior.
Hephaestus	2	god	B	Blacksmith god. Made Achilles' armor. Married Aphrodite.
Hera	1	goddess	A	Zeus' wife.
Heracles	17	demigod	A	Bravest hero of all time.
Hermes	13	god	A	Messenger god. Called the Lord of Wayfaring.

Character	Chapter	Type	Level	Description
Hippolyta	15	demigod	C	Sister of Penthesilea. Accidentally killed by her sister.
Idomeneus	2	man	C	King of Crete. Fought alongside the Greeks.
Iris	13	goddess	B	Messenger goddess. Called the Lady of the Rainbow.
King of Delos	14	man	C	Father of three princesses with supernatural powers.
Laocoön	18	man	B	High priest of Poseidon. Warned the Trojans about the horse. Got crushed by sea monsters.
Laocoön's sons	18	man	C	Crushed by sea monsters along with their father.
Lycomedes	2	man	C	King of Scyros. Hid Achilles from the Greeks.
Machaon	5	man	B	Healer of the Greeks.
Memnon	14	man	B	Ethiopian king who brought an army to assist the Trojans. Called Son of the Bright Dawn.
Menelaus	1	man	A	King of Sparta. His wife, Helen, was stolen by the Trojan, Paris. He rounded up the Greeks for war.
Meriones	12	man	C	Greek warrior.
Nestor	2	man	C	Greek warrior and king of Pylos. Oldest and wisest of the Greeks.
Odysseus	1	man	A	King of Ithaca. Known for his cleverness.

Character	Chapter	Type	Level	Description
Oenone	1	nymph	B	Wood nymph. Loves Paris.
Palamedes	18	man	C	Killed by Odysseus.
Pan	8	god	B	God with goat-legs.
Pandarus	5	man	C	Warrior and prince. Ally of Troy. Wounded Menelaus. Killed by Diomedes.
Paris	1	man	A	Prince of Troy. Judges which goddess gets the golden apple. Steals Helen from Menelaus and thus incites the Trojan war.
Patroclus	2	man	B	Greek warrior. Achilles' best friend.
Pedasus	10	horse	C	Horse belonging to Achilles.
Peleus	1	man	C	King of the Myrmidons. Married Thetis.
Penelope	1	woman	B	Odysseus' wife and Helen's cousin.
Penthesilea	14	woman	B	Amazon queen and warrior. Became a warrior after accidentally killing her sister.
Philoctetes	17	man	B	Greek warrior abandoned on the island of Lemnos with a fearsome injury.
Phoenix	6	man	C	Greek warrior. Achilles' former tutor.
Polydamas	16	man	C	Trojan warrior.
Poseidon	9	god	A	Greek god of the sea, earthquakes, and horses.
Priam	1	man	A	King of Troy.

Character	Chapter	Type	Level	Description
Protesilaus	3	man	C	Greek warrior. First Greek to die in the war.
Queen of Egypt	14	woman	C	Gave a sleeping drug to Helen many years earlier.
Rhesus	7	man	C	King of Thrace. Ally of the Trojans. Owns the finest horses in the Trojan camp.
Sarpedon	5	man	C	Lord of the Lycians. Slain by Patroclus. He was a demigod, being the son of Zeus and a mortal woman.
Sinon	18	man	B	Greek who tricked the Trojans into accepting the horse. Palamedes' armor-bearer.
Sleep	10	god	C	God of sleep. Name was Hypnos (we don't see this in the text).
Thersites	4	man	B	Ugly, bandy-legged Greek warrior. Wants to go home.
Thetis	1	nymph	B	Sea-nymph. Mother of Achilles. Called Thetis of the Silver Feet.
Thrasymedes	14	man	C	Greek warrior. Son of Nestor.
West Wind	10	god	B	Name was Zephyr (not in the text).
Xanthus	10	horse	C	Immortal horse belonging to Achilles. Fathered by the West Wind.
Zeus	1	god	A	One of the most powerful gods. Called All-Father and Thunderer.

Map Work

# on Map	Place	Chapter	Level	Description
1	Aegean Sea	1	A	Troy was on its north-east coast. Separates Troy from Sparta.
2	Argos	2	C	Land of many horses ruled by Diomedes.
3	Aulis Harbor	2	C	Agamemnon's harbor.
4	Black Sea	1	A	Ships sailing there brought trade to Troy.
5	Crete	2	A	A Greek island.
6	Delos	14	C	Island home of three princesses with supernatural powers.
7	Greece	1	A	Group of city-states in the region of the Aegean Sea.
8	Ida	1	C	Mount Ida is where Paris was raised.
9	Ithaca	1	B	A rocky island.
10	Lemnos	17	C	Island where Philoctetes had been abandoned.
11	Mycenae	2	B	Mycenae of the Lion Gate is where Agamemnon's throne was.
12	Olympus	1	B	Mount Olympus is where the gods live.
13	Pylos	2	C	Nestor was king of Pylos.
14	Pytho	2	C	A rocky place.
15	River Thermodon	15	C	River that watered the land of the Amazons.
16	Salamis	2	C	Ajax was Lord of Salamis.
17	Scyros	2	C	Island where Thetis tried to hide Achilles.
18	Sparta	1	A	City on the Aegean Sea.

# on Map	Place	Chapter	Level	Description
N/A	Styx	2	N/A	River in the underworld.
19	Tenedos	18	C	Island behind which the Greek ships were hidden so that the horse could be presented to the Trojans.
20	Thessaly	2	C	Home of Chiron the Centaur.
21	Thisbe	2	C	"Where the wild doves croon"
22	Thrace	7	C	Rhesus was king of Thrace.
23	Troy	1	A	Great city on a hill, surrounded by strong walls.
24	Xanthus River	9	C	River beside which Hector lay after being wounded in battle.

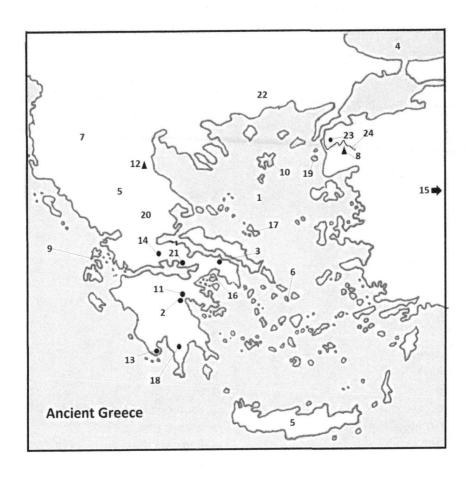

Ancient Greece

Relaxed Study Guide Answer Key

Chapter 1
1. a
2. a, c, d
3. c
4. tall, handsome, selfish, spoiled, strong, irresistible
5. b
6. woman
7. Helen; Menelaus
8. d

Chapter 2
1. b
2. Thetis; nymph; Peleus
3. Styx, heel
4. c
5. a

Chapter 3
1. nine
2. d
3. c
4. Greece; Troy
5. a
6. b

Chapter 4
1. dream
2. Paris; Menelaus
3. e
4. b
5. c
6. b
7. a

Chapter 5
1. e
2. Greeks
3. b
4. a
5. cowardly
6. b
7. c

Chapter 6
1. c
2. Agamemnon
3. Hector; Ajax
4. No one
5. b
6. d
7. Achilles
8. c

Chapter 7
1. a
2. Diomedes; Odysseus
3. Dolon; spy
4. lions; wolf
5. b
6. b

Chapter 8
1. Red rain
2. b
3. b
4. foot; ribs or chest
5. a
6. b
7. d

Chapter 9
1. b
2. a
3. c
4. b
5. Poseidon; monsters; ocean & earthquakes
6. Hector
7. b
8. b

Chapter 10
1. Patroclus
2. d
3. immortal
4. Patroclus; Achilles
5. d
6. b, c, e
7. b
8. d
9. Greeks, Trojans, dogs
10. b
11. Trojans

Chapter 11
1. d
2. b
3. d
4. Breastplate & shin guards made of bronze, silver, tin, and gold; Tall crested helmet of red gold; Shield inlaid with precious metals showing pictures of cities, seas, battles, a lion hunt, fields full of corn, vineyards, and men and women dancing.
5. b
6. Xanthus

7. d
8. b

Chapter 12
1. Hector
2. b
3. c
4. Patroclus' body burned with locks of hair for all as well as slain cattle, slain Trojans, 4 horses, and 2 dogs. His ashes are put in a golden cup in a vault. Then they had chariot races, boxing, wrestling, a foot race, and a spear fight. At the end there was a feast.
5. Hector; Patroclus; 3; 12
6. b

Chapter 13
1. Thetis; Hector
2. d
3. b
4. a, e, h
5. d

Chapter 14
1. d
2. c
3. Palladium or Luck of Troy
4. a
5. c
6. Odysseus
7. d

Chapter 15
1. b
2. b

3. b

Chapter 16
1. b
2. d
3. b, c
4. Antilochus
5. Achilles
6. b
7. a
8. Thetis; Odysseus or Ajax;
Trojans/prisoners; Odysseus
9. b
10. Ajax; Dionysius; sheep;
himself

Chapter 17
1. b
2. Greeks; Lemnos; dragon; foot;
healed

3. c
4. Paris
5. d
6. d

Chapter 18
1. cunning or wit
2. b
3. a
4. c
5. b
6. Laocoön; sons; Athene;
Laocoön; horse
7. d

Chapter 19
1. red fire; shorebird
2. b.
3. d
4. c

A special thank-you to my beta-version readers, Crystal Nelson, Doreen Alcorn, Ariana DiMartino, and Jennifer Kennedy, and my editor, Amy Alcorn.

for more SneakerBlossom Study Guides please visit

sneakerblossom.com

Made in the USA
Monee, IL
27 May 2024

58846206R00083